SECOND EDITION

Super Practice Book

2

SUPER PRACTICE

Emma Szlachta · **Garan Holcombe**

CAMBRIDGE
UNIVERSITY PRESS

Map of the Book

There's / There are

The classroom is a mess. Let's clean it up.

Good idea.

There are some pencils and some pens …

… and **there are** some books. Let's put them in the bookcase.

There's a ball. Let's put it in the cabinet.

Thank you. That's fantastic!

1 **Look and match.**

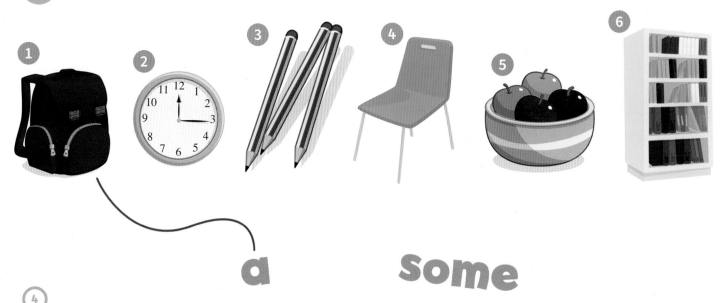

a   some

2 Write *is* or *are*.

1 There ___is___ a red book.

2 There _____ some pencils.

3 There _____ an apple.

4 There _____ a clock.

5 There _____ some candies.

6 There _____ a green pen.

3 Write *There are some* or *There is a*.

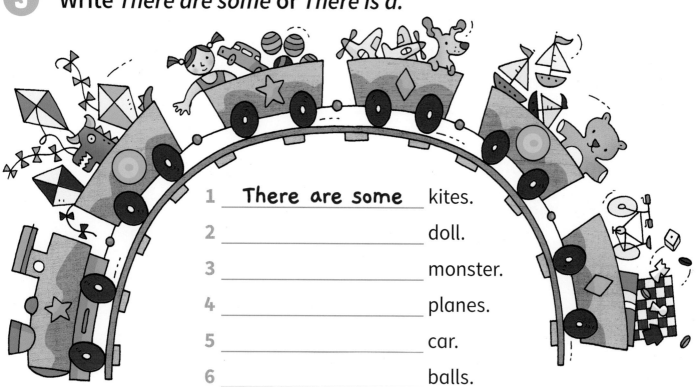

1 ___There are some___ kites.

2 _____ doll.

3 _____ monster.

4 _____ planes.

5 _____ car.

6 _____ balls.

Imperatives

It's good to see you all again. **Stand** up, please.

Don't open your books.

Put your pens in your pencil case. Let's play a game.

Language Focus

Use **imperatives** to give instructions.

Stand up.   *Don't* stand up.

Sit down.   *Don't* sit down.

Put your book in your bag.   *Don't* close your books.

---

1   **Read and complete the sentences.**

1 Open __your books__.

2 Sit _____.

3 Stand _____.

4 C_____ your bag.

5 Pass me y_____ r ru_____ r.

6 Don't o_____ y_____ r bags.

2 Complete the dialogue with the words from the box.

Pass   open   down   Don't   up   ~~sit~~

Mrs. Brown   Hello, class. Welcome back! It's good to see you all again. OK,
(1) _____sit_____ down, please, and (2) _____ your books.

Matt   Oh, no! I don't have a pencil! (3) _____ me a pencil,
please, Sally.

Sally   Shhh, Matt. Here you go.

Matt   Mrs. Brown, I can't see the board.

Mrs. Brown   Stand (4) _____,
Matt. (5) _____
sit down there. Sit
(6) _____ here.

Matt   Thank you.

3 Write the instructions.

1 Don't sit down. _____

2 _____

3 _____

4 _____

5 _____

6 _____

Reading: A Poem

1 Read the poem and write *t* (true) or *f* (false).

A Poem About My Desk

The classroom is a mess.

Look at my desk!

There are some pens and a book.

An apple and a clock.

There are some pencils and a sausage!

A sausage? A sausage!

Don't sit down, Sue and Dan.

Put the pencils in your pencil case
and the sausage in your bag.

Don't sit down, Anna and Alex.

Put the clock on the wall
and the apple in your desk.

Don't sit down. Let's clean up this mess.

1 The classroom isn't clean. ☑ t

2 There are two books. ☐

3 There's a banana. ☐

4 There's a clock. ☐

5 There are some pencils. ☐

6 There isn't a sausage. ☐

1 **What is on your desk? Write a list.**

There's a _____

_____

_____

_____

_____

There are some _____

_____

_____

_____

_____

2 **Write a poem about your desk. Then draw it.**

A Poem About My Desk

The classroom is a mess.

Look at my desk!

There are _____

_____

_____

_____

_____

Look at my desk!

Don't sit down. Let's clean up this mess.

Listening: In the Classroom

1 🎧 01 **Listen and number the pictures.**

a □

b □

c □

d **1**

e □

f □

2 🎧 02 **Listen and check ✓ the correct sentence.**

1 □ Sit down, please.   ✓ Don't sit down, please.

2 □ Stand up, please.   □ Don't stand up.

3 □ Get your books, please.   □ Don't get your books.

4 □ Get your crayons, please.   □ Don't get your crayons.

5 □ Write your name, please.   □ Don't write your name.

1 **What's in your bag? Draw five things and say.**

There's a pencil case. There are three books. There's a notebook.

2 **Work with a friend. Talk about your bags.
Play the memory game.**

There's a pencil case in your bag.

Yes! What color is it?

It's blue.

Yes, that's right!

3 **Talk about your friend's bag.**

In Pablo's bag, there's a blue pencil case. There are three books. One is yellow . . .

1 Telling the Time

Language Focus

Use **What time is it?** to ask the time and **It's ... o'clock** to answer.

Use **When do you ... ?** to ask about the time of an activity and **At ... o'clock** to answer.

What time is it?	*It's nine o'clock.*
When do you have breakfast?	*At seven o'clock.*

1 Read and match.

1 What time is it? It's two o'clock.   **b**

2 When do you have lunch? At twelve o'clock. ☐

3 What time is it? It's ten o'clock. ☐

4 When do you go to bed? At eight o'clock. ☐

5 What time is it? It's four o'clock. ☐

6 When do you get up? At six o'clock. ☐

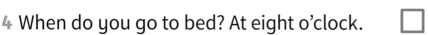

2 **Complete the dialogue with the words from the box.**

~~time~~   ten   do   When   at   o'clock

Mary   Tell me about your day. What **(1)** ___time___ do you get up?

Alan   OK. Well, I get up **(2)** _____ seven o'clock.

Mary   **(3)** _____ do you go to school?

Alan   At nine **(4)** _____ .

Mary   And when **(5)** _____ you play in the park?

Alan   On Saturday at **(6)** _____ o'clock.

3 **Write sentences.**

1 I ___get up at___
___six o'clock___ .

2 I _____
_____ .

3 I _____
_____ .

4 I _____
_____ .

5 I _____
_____ .

6 I _____
_____ .

Simple Present, 3rd Person

Eva **gets up** at seven o'clock.

She **goes** to school at eight o'clock.

She **has** lunch at twelve o'clock.

She **brushes** her teeth, and then she **goes** to bed at eight o'clock.

Language Focus

Use the **simple present, 3rd person (gets**, **goes)** to talk about what other people do.

*Eva **gets up** at seven o'clock.*   *She **goes** to school at eight o'clock.*

1   **Match the sentences with the pictures.**

1 He has dinner at six o'clock with his family.   ☑ d

2 He goes to work at eight o'clock at night.   ☐

3 He comes home at six o'clock in the morning.   ☐

4 He has breakfast at seven o'clock.   ☐

5 He plays in the park at eight o'clock.   ☐

6 He goes to bed at nine o'clock in the evening.   ☐

a

b

c

d

e

f

2 Match to complete the sentences.

1 Emma gets   a breakfast and
                     brushes her teeth.

2 Kate has   b to bed at eight o'clock.

3 Dan gets   c her teeth in the morning and in the evening.

4 Hugo goes   d up at nine o'clock on Saturdays, and she plays soccer.

5 Lucy brushes   e in the park after school.

6 Fred plays   f dressed in jeans and a T-shirt.

3 Complete the text with the words from the box.

has   leaves   arrives   gets   starts   ~~works~~

Alison is a teacher. She
(1) ___works___ in a big school in
New York. In the morning, she
(2) _____ the house at seven
o'clock and (3) _____ at
school at eight o'clock. She
(4) _____ two classes in the
morning, and then she has lunch.
She (5) _____ her afternoon
class at one o'clock, and the children
go home at four o'clock. She leaves
school at six o'clock and
(6) _____ home and has
dinner. What a long day!

Reading: A Blog Entry

1 **Read the text. Circle the correct words.**

My Blog — by Suzy James

My Mom

My mom is fantastic! She gets up at six o'clock and walks me and my brother to school at eight o'clock. Then she goes to work on the bus. She has a busy day at work, and she has lunch at her desk. Then at four o'clock, she gets me and my brother from school, and she helps me with my homework. She cooks, and we all have dinner at five o'clock. On Fridays, we have pizza. It's my favorite dinner. I go to bed at eight o'clock, and Mom goes to bed at ten o'clock. She has a long day.

1 Mom gets up at *six* / *eight* o'clock.

2 She *walks* / *takes the bus* to work.

3 She has lunch at *her desk* / *one o'clock*.

4 She *works some more* / *helps Suzy with her homework* at home.

5 *Mom has* / *They all have* dinner at five o'clock.

6 *Suzy* / *Mom* goes to bed at ten o'clock.

1 Write notes about your mom or dad. Use the words from the box.

> ~~get up~~   have breakfast   go to work   have lunch
> start work   leave work   get home   watch TV   go to bed

Dad gets up at seven o'clock.

2 Write about your mom or dad. What does she / he do?

My Blog

Listening: Daily Routines

1  **Listen and check ☑ the correct clock.**

1 Eva gets up at …   **a** ☑   **b** ☐

2 Eva has breakfast at …   **a** ☐   **b** ☐

3 Eva goes to school at …   **a** ☐   **b** ☐

4 Eva has lunch at …   **a** ☐   **b** ☐

5 Eva has dinner at …   **a** ☐   **b** ☐

6 Eva goes to bed at …   **a** ☐   **b** ☐

2 **Listen and circle *yes* or *no*.**

1 Dan gets home at four o'clock.   (yes)/ no

2 Dan walks home with his mom and his sister.   yes / no

3 At five o'clock, Dan plays with his sister.   yes / no

4 Dan has dinner at seven o'clock.   yes / no

5 After dinner, Dan, his sister, and his dad read a story.   yes / no

6 After the story, Dan brushes his teeth and goes to bed.   yes / no

1 **Look at Mindy's day. Choose a picture and say. Play the guessing game.**

> Mindy has dinner at seven o'clock.

> Number 5!

get up

have breakfast

have lunch

play in the park

have dinner

go to bed

2 **Draw a picture of your favorite activity to do on the weekend. Complete and practice.**

On the weekend, I
_____ at _____
o'clock. It's my favorite activity!

3 **Show your picture to a friend. Talk about your favorite activity to do on the weekend.**

> Look. This is me on the weekend. I play computer games at five o'clock. What about you?

> I ride my bike in the park. I go there at eleven o'clock.

2 likes / doesn't like

Eva **likes** sandwiches at lunchtime. She **doesn't like** cheese on her sandwich. She **likes** sausages.

Eva **likes** bananas and orange juice for breakfast.

Eva has dinner at five o'clock. She **likes** chicken and carrots. She **doesn't like** peas.

Eva has dessert at seven o'clock. She **likes** milk and cookies.

Language Focus

Use **likes** and **doesn't like** to talk about preferences.

*Freddy **likes** spiders. Freddy **doesn't like** apples.*

---

1 Circle the correct words to complete the sentences.

1 Tony *likes* / *doesn't like* carrots.

2 Ben *likes* / *doesn't like* apples.

3 Mary *likes* / *doesn't like* cheese.

4 Monica *likes* / *doesn't like* bananas.

5 Bill *likes* / *doesn't like* peas.

6 Tim *likes* / *doesn't like* chicken.

a

b

c

d

e

f

2 Complete the text with the words from the box.

likes   ~~likes~~   doesn't   likes   likes   like

The zoo is busy. There are lots of animals. It's six o'clock, and the animals are having breakfast. The zebra (1) ____likes____ apples, but he (2) _____ like bananas. The monkey (3) _____ yellow bananas for breakfast, and the tiger (4) _____ steak. The snake doesn't (5) _____ peas. He (6) _____ big rats for breakfast. Yum!

3 Complete the sentences.

1 Emma **doesn't like carrots** .

2 Mark _____ .

3 Suzy _____ .

4 Dan _____ .

5 Pam _____ .

6 Toby _____ .

Does . . . like . . . ?

Does Dexter sleep all day?

Does Peggy **like** Dexter?

Does Peggy speak?

Hello, Eva!

Yes, he does. He **likes** his bed!

No, she doesn't!

Yes, she does!

Language Focus

Use **Does . . . like . . . ?** to ask questions about what people like.

Use **Yes, he / she does** and **No, he / she doesn't** to give short answers.

***Does** Mark **like** bananas?*   **Yes, he does.** / **No, he doesn't.**

1 **Write *Yes, he / she does* or *No, he / she doesn't.***

1 Does Anna like sausages? <u>**Yes, she does**</u>. They're her favorite.

2 Does Bill walk to school? _____. He rides his bike.

3 Does May like cats? _____. She likes dogs.

4 Does your mom get up at six o'clock? _____, but not on weekends.

5 Does your parrot like carrots? _____. He likes apples.

6 Does your dad go to work every day? _____. He arrives at nine o'clock.

2 Complete the dialogue with the words from the box.

he ~~Does~~ walk she does doesn't

Toby (1) _____**Does**_____ your mom get up early?

Katy Yes, (2) _____ does.
She goes to work every day.

Toby Does she (3) _____ to work?

Katy No, she (4) _____. She rides a bike.

Toby Does she have lunch at work?

Katy Yes, she (5) _____. She has a sandwich and some fruit.

Toby Does your dad ride a bike to work, too?

Katy No, (6) _____ doesn't. He drives a car.

3 Write questions and answers.

1 sausages / Mark / Does / like / ?
Does Mark like sausages? ✓ **Yes, he does.**

2 ride / Ben / school / a bike / Does / to / ?
_____ ✓ _____

3 chicken / the zebra / eat / Does / ?
_____ ✗ _____

4 Does / swimming / like / the hippo / ?
_____ ✗ _____

5 a lot / cat / your / Does / sleep / ?
_____ ✓ _____

6 eight o'clock / Tina / go to / Does / bed / at / ?
_____ ✗ _____

Reading: A Web Page

1 **Read the text and answer the questions.**

| Home | Our Animals | Contact Us | Opening Times |

BLUEWATER ZOO

The Hippos

This is Hugo the hippo. He's 15 years old and lives at the zoo. He's from Africa. He has a big house and water to swim in. He gets up early in the morning, but he likes naps after lunch. He likes fruit. His favorite food is apples, but he doesn't like carrots! Does he like the water? Yes, he does, and he can swim.

Hannah lives with Hugo. Hugo and Hannah are good friends. Hannah likes the water, too, but she doesn't like apples. She likes bananas. Come and visit Hugo and Hannah! We are open from nine o'clock to five o'clock every day.

1 Where is Hugo from?   He's from Africa.

2 Does Hugo get up early?   _____

3 Does he nap in the morning? _____

4 What's his favorite food?   _____

5 Can Hugo swim?   _____

6 Does Hannah like the water? _____

1 **Write notes about Terry the tiger. Use the words from the box.**

eight   a long tail   ~~India~~   steak   carrots   run fast

Terry comes from **(1)** _____India_____ .
He's **(2)** _____ years old.
He likes **(3)** _____ .
He doesn't like **(4)** _____ .
He can **(5)** _____ .
He has **(6)** _____ .

2 **Write about Terry the tiger. Use your notes from Activity 1.**

_____

_____

_____

_____

_____

_____

_____

_____

_____

Listening: My Favorite Animal

1 🎧 05 **Listen and match the children with the animals they like.**

1 Alex
2 Grace
3 Tom
4 Kim
5 Jill
6 Nick

a
b
c
d
e
f

2 🎧 06 **Listen and circle the correct answers.**

1 Does Holly's mom like crocodiles? (a) Yes, she does. b No, she doesn't.
2 Does her dad like zebras? a Yes, he does. b No, he doesn't.
3 Does her brother like snakes? a Yes, he does. b No, he doesn't.
4 Does her sister like snakes? a Yes, she does. b No, she doesn't.
5 Does Holly like parrots? a Yes, she does. b No, she doesn't.
6 Does Holly like monkeys? a Yes, she does. b No, she doesn't.

1 **Work with a friend. Look at the photos. Play the guessing game.**

monkey

Does it live in trees?

Yes, it does.

Can it fly?

No, it can't.

Is it the monkey?

Yes, it is!

elephant

parrot

bear

spider

fish

2 **With your friend, talk about the animals in Activity 1.**

Do you like monkeys?

Yes, I do! Do you like elephants?

3 **Which animals does your friend like or not like? Say.**

Emma likes monkeys, but she doesn't like parrots. She really likes bears and …

3 Does...have...?

Does your town **have** a hospital?

Does your town **have** a movie theater?

No, it doesn't.

Yes, it does.

Language Focus

Use **Does . . . have . . . ?** to ask about possessions and places.

Use **Yes, it does** and **No, it doesn't** to give short answers.

Does your town **have** a swimming pool?   **Yes, it does.**

Does your town **have** a train station?   **No, it doesn't.**

1   **Write Yes, he does or No, he doesn't.**

1 Does Ben have a book? <u>Yes, he does.</u>

2 Does he have a bike? _____

3 Does he have a cat? _____

4 Does he have a notebook? _____

5 Does he have a kite? _____

6 Does he have a jacket? _____

Ben

2 **Look and write questions and answers.**

1 _Does Top Town have_ a train station?   Yes, it does.

2 Does Top Town have a school?   _____.

3 _____ a hospital?   No, it doesn't.

4 Does Top Town have a café?   _____.

5 Does Top Town have a park?   _____.

6 _____ a swimming pool?   No, it doesn't.

3 **Write questions and answers.**

1 town / your / Does / a movie theater / have / ?

Does your town have a movie theater? ✓ _Yes, it does._

2 your / a store / Does / town / have / ?

_____ ✓ _____

3 a dog / Anna / have / Does / ?

_____ ✗ _____

4 Tim / a go-kart / have / Does / ?

_____ ✗ _____

5 a playground / Does / have / your town / ?

_____ ✓ _____

6 your town / a hospital / have / Does / ?

_____ ✗ _____

29

Prepositions

Where is the movie theater?

It's between the café and the fruit store.

Language Focus

Use **prepositions** to describe where things and places are.

*The movie theater is **between** the toy store and Green Street.*

*The hospital is **behind** the playground.*

*The school is **in front of** the park.*

*The café is **next to** the train station.*

1 **Circle the correct words to complete the sentences.**

1 The books are (next to) / *behind* the apple.

2 The apple is *in front of* / *between* the books and the pencils.

3 The ruler is *in front of* / *behind* the clock.

4 The fish is *on* / *in* the water.

5 The red book is *between* / *next to* the fish and the clock.

6 The blue book is *on* / *under* the yellow book.

2 **Match the sentences with the pictures.**

1 The cat is next to the dog. [e]

2 The cat is in front of the dog. ☐

3 The cat is between the dog and the ball. ☐

4 The cat is on the ball. ☐

5 The cat is behind the ball. ☐

6 The cat is under the ball. ☐

3 **Look and write the words.**

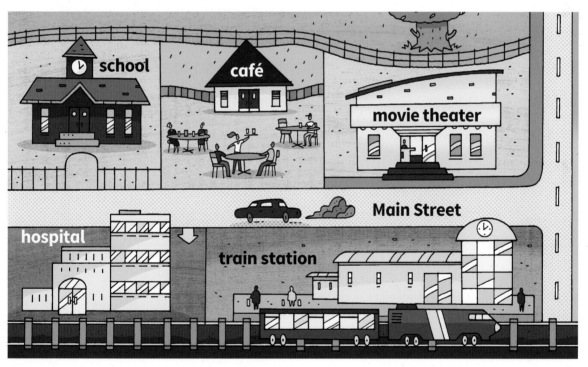

1 The school is _____next to_____ the café.

2 The car is _____ the café.

3 The café is _____ the movie theater.

4 The train is _____ the train station.

5 The tree is _____ the movie theater.

6 The café is _____ the school and the movie theater.

Reading: A Letter

1 **Read the text. Circle the correct words.**

Hi James,

My favorite days of the week are Saturday and Sunday.
On Saturdays, my mom takes me and my brother to the
swimming pool in the morning. We go every week, and
we have lots of fun. After that, we go to the café next to
the swimming pool for lunch. I have a sandwich, and my
brother has pizza. On Sundays, we go to the park behind
our house, and we play soccer. Sometimes we go to the
movie theater in town. It isn't a big movie theater, but
it shows movies for children on Sunday mornings. My
favorite movies are about animals.

Does your town have a swimming pool? What's your
favorite day of the week?

Freddie

1 Freddie *likes* / *doesn't like* the weekend.

2 Freddie goes to the *movie theater* / *swimming pool* on Saturday mornings.

3 He eats *pizza* / *a sandwich* for lunch.

4 The park is behind *the movie theater* / *his house.*

5 The movie theater *is* / *isn't* small.

6 Freddie *likes* / *doesn't like* movies about animals.

1 Write a list of places in your town. What can you do there?

_____

_____

_____

_____

_____

_____

_____

_____

2 Write a letter to Freddie. Tell him about your favorite days and where you go in your town.

_____

_____

_____

_____

_____

_____

_____

_____

Listening: Places

1 🎧07 Listen and check ☑ or put an X ☒.

Places	Sam's Town	Hugo's Town
1	✓	
2		
3		
4		
5		

2 🎧08 Listen and draw lines.

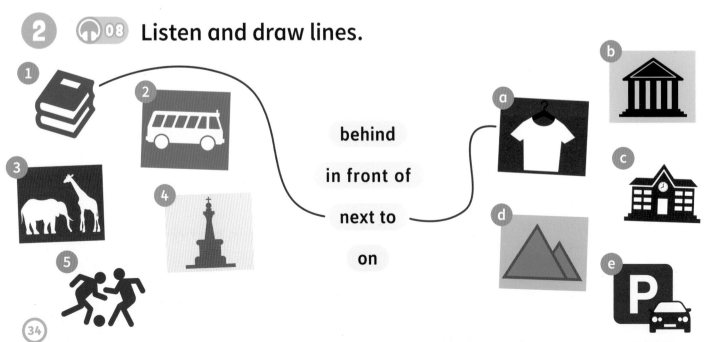

behind

in front of

next to

on

1 Choose five places to complete the map of the town. Give your town a name.

sports center
museum
train station
swimming pool
market
movie theater
hospital
playground

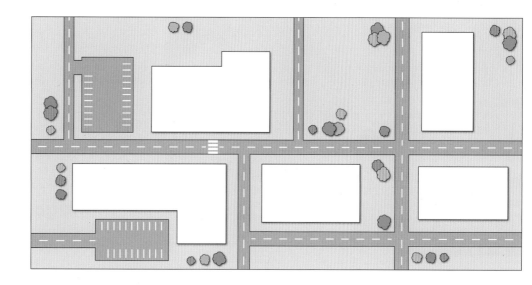

Name of Town: _____

2 Work with a friend. Which places does your friend's town have? Ask and check ☑ your friend's town's places in Activity 1.

What's the name of your town?

It's Super Town.

Does your town have a sports center?

No, it doesn't. Does your town have a hospital?

Yes, it does.

3 Work with a friend. Where are the places on your maps? Ask and answer.

Where's the sports center in your town?

It's next to the train station.

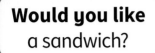

Would you like a sandwich?

Would you like some tomatoes?

Would you **like** a mango?

Would you like some grapes?

Yes, please.

No, thank you.

No, thank you.

Yes, please.

Language Focus

Use **Would you like . . . ?** to ask polite questions. Use **Yes, please** and **No, thank you** to give polite short answers.

Would you like *a tomato?*   **Yes, please.**

Would you like *some bread?*   **No, thank you.**

1   **Look and write** *some* **or** *an.*

1	**some**	watermelon	5	_____	apple
2	_____	egg	6	_____	mango
3	_____	cake	7	_____	bread
4	_____	grapes			

2 **Complete the dialogue with the words from the box.**

| a | some | please | ~~like~~ | Would | No |

Dad Would you **(1)** ___like___ a sandwich, Sally?

Sally Yes, **(2)** _____ .

Dad **(3)** _____ you like a sausage on your sandwich?

Sally **(4)** _____ , thank you. I'd like **(5)** _____ cheese.

Dad Would you like an apple or **(6)** _____ banana, too?

Sally Yes, please. A banana.

3 **Look and write questions and answers.**

1 ___Would you like a mango?___ ✓ Yes, please.

2 _____ some grapes? ✗

  No, _____ .

3 _____ apple? ✗

  _____ thank you.

4 _____ ? ✓

  Yes, _____ .

5 _____ ? ✓

  _____ .

6 _____ ? ✗

  _____ .

ⓐ   ⓑ

ⓒ   ⓓ

ⓔ   ⓕ

Are there / Is there any . . . ?

Is there any milk in the fridge?

Are there any lemons?

Is there any chicken in the fridge?

No, there isn't.

No, there aren't any.

Yes, there is.

Language Focus

Use **Is there any . . . ?** and **Are there any . . . ?** to ask about singular and plural nouns. Use **Yes, there is / are** and **No, there isn't / aren't any** to give short answers.

Are there any pears in the fridge?   *Yes, there are.*

No, there aren't any.

Is there any bread in the basket?   *Yes, there is.*

No, there isn't any.

1   **Look and write.**

1 Are there any bananas?   No, there aren't any.

2 Is there any bread?   _____

3 Are there any tomatoes?   _____

4 Is there any fish?   _____

5 Are there any grapes?   _____

6 Are there any pears?   _____

38

2 **Write numbers to put the dialogue in order.**

Mia	Are there any sausages?	☐
John	Yes, there are. There are two sausages.	☐
John	Yes, there is. There's white bread. Let's look in the fridge.	☐
Mia	OK. Is there any chicken?	☐
Mia	My favorite – a sausage sandwich. Is there any cake?	☐
John	Yes, there is. There's chocolate cake. Yummy!	☐
Mia	Let's make sandwiches for lunch. Is there any bread?	1
John	No, there isn't any.	☐

3 **Write questions.**

1 Are / any / there / potatoes / the basket / in / ?

Are there any potatoes in the basket?

2 there / Is / cake / any / ?

_____

3 there / lemons / Are / any / ?

_____

4 there / cheese / in / Is / the fridge / any / ?

_____

5 the basket / Is / any / bread / there / in / ?

_____

6 there / Are / apples / in / the fridge / any / ?

_____

Reading: A Recipe

1 Look. Then answer the questions about the recipe.

milk   butter   lemon   chocolate

egg   flour   frying pan

PANCAKES

1. Put a cup of flour in a bowl.
2. Put an egg and a cup of milk in the bowl. Start mixing.
3. Put one tablespoon of butter in a frying pan.
4. Put some of the mixture in the frying pan.
5. Fry the pancake for two minutes each side. (Can you flip the pancake?!)
6. Put chocolate, fruit, or lemon juice on your pancake.

Enjoy the pancakes with your friends.

1 How many cups of flour are there?   **There is one cup of flour.**

2 How many eggs are there? _____

3 Is there any water? _____

4 Is there any butter? _____

5 Is there any fruit? _____

6 What else can you put on the pancake? _____

1 What food would you like to make? Write a list of things you would need to make it.

_____

_____

_____

_____

_____

_____

_____

_____

2 Write a recipe for your food.

_____

_____

_____

_____

_____

_____

Listening: Fruit, Vegetables, and Eggs!

1 🎧 09 **Listen and number the pictures.**

a

☐

b

☐

c

☐

d

☐

e

1

f

☐

2 🎧 10 **What would they like? Listen and match.**

1 Lucy

2 Connor

3 Anna

4 Jack

5 May

a

b

c

d

e

1 **What do you have for your picnic? Draw five things and say.**

> For my picnic, there are some sandwiches, some grapes, some potato chips, and some tomatoes. To drink, there's some juice.

2 **Work with a friend. Talk about your picnic food and drinks.**

> There are some sandwiches for my picnic.

> How many sandwiches are there?

> There are three sandwiches.

3 **What would your friend like at your picnic? Ask and answer.**

> Would you like a sandwich?

> Yes, please! Would you like an apple?

> No, thank you. I don't like apples.

5 this, that, these, those

Language Focus

Use **this** and **these** to talk about singular (this) and plural (these) things that are near to you. Use **that** and **those** to talk about singular (that) and plural (those) things that are far from you.

*I like **this** book.*   *I like **that** book.*

*I like **these** books.*   *I like **those** books.*

---

1 **Circle the correct words to complete the sentences.**

1 I like (this) / these lamp.

2 I don't like these / this yellow chairs.

3 Do you like these / those blue chairs?

4 I like that / those lamp.

5 I like these / this blue jeans.

6 Do you like that / this red hat?

2 Match the sentences with the pictures.

1 I like this hat. `e`
2 I don't like these shoes. ☐
3 I like those shoes. ☐
4 I don't like that jacket. ☐
5 I don't like that hat. ☐
6 I like this jacket. ☐

f

e

a b c d

3 Look and write *this*, *that*, *these*, or *those*.

Do you like (1) ___**these**___ yellow shoes?

No, I don't. I like (2) _____ green shoes.

Look at (3) _____ hats over there.

Do you like (4) _____ red hat?

Yes, I do.

I like (5) _____ red T-shirt. Do you?

Yes, I do. I like this blue shirt, too.

Do you like (6) _____ shoes over there?

No, I don't. They're awful!

Whose … is this? / Whose … are these?

Whose socks are these?

They're Sam's. He's my brother.

Whose car is this? Is it yours?

No, it's Sam's, too.

Whose brother is this?!

Sam! What are you doing under the bed?

Language Focus

Use **Whose … are these?** to ask about possession of plural items.

Use **Whose … is this?** to ask about possession of singular items.

Whose socks *are these?*   *They're* Fred's.

Whose hat *is this?*   *It's* May's.

1 Circle the correct words to complete the sentences.

1 **A** Whose hat is this?
  B It's *Claire* / *Claire's*.

2 **A** Whose socks are *these* / *this*?
  B They're Bob's.

3 **A** Whose pencil is this?
  B It's *my* / *mine*.

4 Whose jeans are these? Are they *yours* / *your*?

5 *Whose* / *Who's* doll is this? Is it Jane's?

6 Whose soccer shoes are these? Are they *Tom's* / *Toms*?

2 **Look and write the names.**

1 Whose purple socks are those? **They're May's.**

2 Whose soccer ball is that? _____

3 Whose plane is that? _____

4 Whose hat is that? _____

5 Whose black socks are those? _____

6 Whose white shoes are those? _____

3 **Complete the dialogue with the words from the box.**

| they're   ~~Whose~~   yours   mine   's   these |

Mrs. Bush What a mess! Let's clean up the classroom. **(1)** _____**Whose**_____ pen is this?

Tim It's **(2)** _____, Mrs. Bush.

Mrs. Bush And whose pencil case is this? Is it **(3)** _____, Alice?

Alice No, it's not mine. It's Tim **(4)** _____.

Mrs. Bush OK. Whose socks are **(5)** _____ under the desk? Are they yours, Tim?

Tim Sorry, Mrs. Bush. Yes, **(6)** _____ mine.

Mrs. Bush Tim! Please clean up your pen, your pencil case, and your socks!

Reading: A Web Page

1 Read the texts and answer the questions.

HOME IDEAS

Home | **Bedrooms** | Living Rooms | Garden | Contact Us

When I want to think, I go to my bedroom. It's my favorite room in the house. My room is blue and green, and I have lots of books. I like books. I don't have a TV or a computer in my bedroom, but that's OK. I can watch TV in the living room. I listen to music in my bedroom, and it's a great place to have fun! Look at those blue, green, and red things on the wall. I can climb in my bedroom!

Alice from England

Ben from Canada

My bedroom is blue. I have some toys, and that's my sister's doll on my bed! I don't have a clock or a bookcase. Can you see that big brown tree on the wall? I look at my tree when I want to think about my vacations. I like climbing trees. I have a cat, Bobby, and he doesn't like the tree! There is no water in my bedroom, but my bed is a boat!

1 There's a boat. Whose bedroom is it?   It's Ben's bedroom.
2 Whose bedroom has a tree in it?
3 Whose bedroom is green and blue?
4 It doesn't have a TV. Whose bedroom is it?
5 Whose bedroom can you climb in?
6 There are toys. Whose bedroom is it?

1 **What is in your bedroom? Write a list.**

_____   _____

_____   _____

_____   _____

_____   _____

_____

2 **Draw and write about your bedroom. What do you like doing there?**

_____

_____

_____

_____

_____

_____

_____

_____

_____

_____

_____

1 🎧 11 **Listen and check ☑ the correct picture.**

1 a ✓ b ☐

2 a ☐ b ☐

3 a ☐ b ☐

4 a ☐ b ☐

5 a ☐ b ☐

6 a ☐ b ☐

2 🎧 12 **Listen and circle *Adam's* or *Lucy's*.**

1 Whose ball is this? *Adam's / (Lucy's)*

2 Whose crayons are these? *Adam's / Lucy's*

3 Whose jeans are these? *Adam's / Lucy's*

4 Whose jacket is this? *Adam's / Lucy's*

5 Whose books are these? *Adam's / Lucy's*

6 Whose kite is this? *Adam's / Lucy's*

1 Draw five things that belong to people in your family. You can draw clothes, toys, furniture, or other things.

2 Work with a friend. Look at your pictures in Activity 1. Ask and answer.

Whose mirror is this?

It's my sister's mirror. Whose shoes are these?

They're my dad's shoes.

3 Talk about your friend's pictures.

My friend is Sue, and this is her sister's mirror. It's beautiful. These are her dad's shoes. They're brown. This …

6 Am / Is / Are + Adjective

Language Focus

Use **Are you** + **adjective?** to ask about how people are feeling.

Use **I'm** + **adjective** to describe how you are feeling.

Are you angry?	*No, I'm not angry.* ***I'm tired.***
Are you happy?	*Yes, I'm happy, and* ***I'm excited.***

1 Look, read, and write the words.

 1 He is
_____sad_____.

 2 She is
_____.

 3 She is
_____.

 4 He is
_____.

 5 She is
_____.

 6 He is
_____.

2 Match the phrases with the pictures.

1 I'm excited.
2 I'm sad.
3 I'm tired.
4 I'm happy.
5 I'm angry.
6 I'm scared.

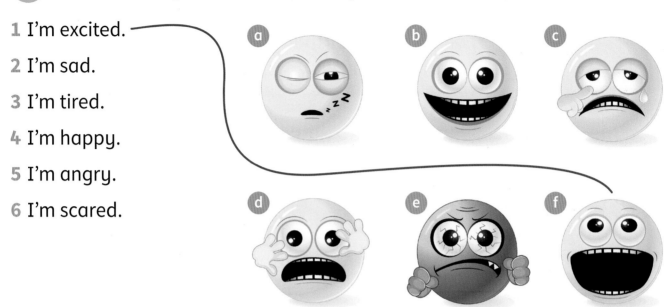

3 Circle the correct words to complete the sentences.

1 Are you angry?
No, I'm not. It's a busy week.
I'm *tired* / *sad*.

2 Are you *excited* / *scared*?
Yes, there's a big dog. Help!

3 Are you *angry* / *happy*?
Yes, I am. It's the weekend!

4 Are you sad?
No, I'm not. I'm *angry* / *excited.* There isn't any cake.

5 Are you *excited* / *tired*?
Yes, I am. It's my birthday party today!

6 Are you tired?
No, I'm not. I'm *happy* / *sad*. I can't play soccer today.

The Months, our, their

Thank you! **Our** birthdays are both in May.

I have an invitation for Sally and Tim, too.

When are **their** birthdays?

Come to Lucy's Party
Saturday May 26
12 Green Road
3 o'clock

Yes! My party is at my house!

Sally's birthday is in July, and Tim's birthday is in October.

Language Focus

Use **our** and **their** before nouns to talk about plural possession.

Our birthdays are both in May.

Their birthdays are in November.

1 **Look and write the months.**

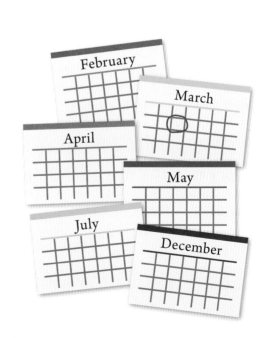

1 My birthday is in **M a** r **c** h.

2 Our birthdays are in __ e __ __ m b __ r.

3 My cat is four. His birthday is in A __ __ i __.

4 My dog is ten. Her birthday is in __ __ l __.

5 Their birthdays are in F __ __ r __ __ r __.

6 His birthday is in __ a __.

2 **Circle the correct words to complete the sentences.**

1 It's Lucy's birthday today. (Her) / *Their* birthday is in May.

2 It's Ben's party today. He's nine. *His* / *He* birthday is in August.

3 My sister is 15 today. *She* / *Her* birthday is in May.

4 I have a present for my dad. *Her* / *His* birthday is in October.

5 We are eight today! *Our* / *Their* birthday is in December.

6 I'm ten today. *My* / *Mine* birthday is in January.

3 **Complete the sentences with the words from the box.**

Her His His My ~~Our~~ Their

1 We are seven. _____**Our**_____ birthdays are in March.

2 I'm four. _____ birthday's today.

3 She's ten. _____ birthday party is today.

4 He's 12. _____ party is at four o'clock.

5 They are six today. _____ birthday is in July.

6 My dog is five today. _____ birthday is in April.

Reading: An Invitation

1 **Read the party invitations. Answer the questions.**

Dear Jenny,

Please come to my party on Sunday, July 14 at one o'clock. My party is in the park. Please bring your swimming things. We can swim in the swimming pool. I have a soccer ball, so we can play soccer, too.
My mom has lots of good food: sandwiches, candy, and cupcakes!

See you on Sunday.

Katy

Dear Ben,

We are seven! Come to our party on Saturday. It starts at four o'clock. It's at Dan's house, 45 West Road (near the swimming pool). We can play games and eat birthday cake.

Don't be late.

See you there!

Dan and Ruby

1 What time is Katy's party? **It's at one o'clock.** _____

2 What month is Katy's party? _____

3 What can you do at Katy's party? _____

4 How old are Dan and Ruby? _____

5 Whose house is Dan and Ruby's party at? _____

6 Where is Dan's house? _____

1 Make notes about your party.

When?	What Time?	Where?	Activities?	Food?
		park	painting soccer	sandwiches

2 Write an invitation. Use your notes from Activity 1.

Listening: Parties

1 🎧 13 **Listen and number the pictures.**

 a ☐

 b ☐

 c ☐

 d ☐

 e 1

 f ☐

2 🎧 14 **Listen and draw lines.**

1 Alex and Dan

2 Kim

3 Pat and Mark

4 Bobby

5 Olivia and Alice

 a

 b

 c

 d

 e

1 **Work with a friend. Plan a class party. Complete the table.**

> Let's bring some balloons to our party.

> Good idea!

> OK. And I'd like to bring some grapes, too.

Things	Food and Drink	Games
balloons	grapes	bingo

2 **With your friend, write your answers. Then practice.**

1 Where is your class party?

   It's _____.

2 What month is your party?

   It's in _____.

3 What day is your party?

   It's on _____.

4 What do you want to do?

   We want to play _____
   and _____.

3 **Talk about your class party.**

> Our party is in the classroom. It's in April, and it's on a Friday. We want to play with balloons, eat cake, and sing.

7 I'd like to . . .

I'd like to go sailing on a big boat.

I'd like to fly to Canada and see a bear.

I'd like to drive a big truck.

Language Focus

Use **I'd like to** + **verb ...** to talk about wishes.

I'd like to go to Africa by plane.

I'd like to drive a train.

1 **Complete the sentences with the words from the box.**

| like | ~~to~~ | to see | I'd | fly | around | eat |

1 I'd like to go ___to___ Canada.

2 I'd _____ to see a snake.

3 _____ like to go to Italy.

4 I'd like to _____ ice cream.

5 I'd like to _____ the world.

6 I'd like _____ a bear.

2 **Circle the correct words to complete the sentences.**

1 I'd like to *(go)* / *sail* to the jungle by bus.

2 I'd *like* / *likes* to eat pizza.

3 I *like* / *'d like* to see an elephant.

4 I'd like to *fly to* / *fly* Africa.

5 I'd like *sail* / *to sail* around the world.

6 I'd like to *drive* / *fly* a bus.

3 **Write sentences using *I'd like to* and the words from the box.**

ride a scooter   fly a helicopter   sail a boat
~~drive a train~~   ride a motorcycle   drive a truck

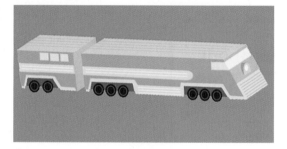

1 <u>I'd like to drive a train.</u>

2 _____

3 _____

4 _____

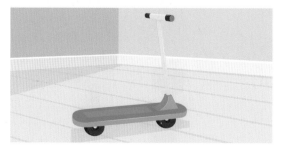

5 _____

6 _____

Verb + ing

What **are** you **doing? Are** you **driving** a car?

No, I'm not.

Are you **driving** a big truck?

Yes, I am!

No, I'm not.

Yes, I am!

What **are** you **doing? Are** you **flying** a plane?

Are you **skateboarding?**

Language Focus

Use **is** / **are** + **verb** + **ing** to ask and answer about actions at the moment of speaking. Use **Yes, I am** and **No, I'm not** to give short answers.

*What **are** you **doing?***	*I**'m flying** a plane.*
*What **is** he **doing?***	*He**'s riding** his bike.*
***Are** you **flying** a plane?*	***Yes, I am.** / **No, I'm not.***

1 **Write *ing* words.**

1 She __'s__ ___listening___ to music. (listen)

2 He _____ _____ breakfast. (eat)

3 I _____ _____ dressed. (get)

4 She _____ _____ ice cream. (eat)

5 He _____ _____ his teeth. (brush)

6 I _____ _____ a photo. (take)

② Write questions.

1 are / What / doing / you / ?

__What are you doing?__

2 soccer / you / Are / playing / ?

_____

3 she / Is / a scooter / riding / ?

_____

4 is / What / doing / she / ?

_____

5 ice cream / Are / eating / you / ?

_____

6 playing / he / Is / computer games / ?

_____

③ Look and write the missing words.

1 What ___are you___ doing?

I __'m looking__ for my jacket.

2 What _____ Lucy doing?

She _____ sailing a boat.

3 What _____ you _____?

I _____ for a bus.

4 What's Ben doing?

He _____ with his cars.

5 _____ Marie doing?

_____ her bike.

6 _____ Dad doing?

_____ the guitar.

Reading: A Postcard

1 **Read the postcards. Check ☑ the activities that Ryan and Dan do. Write R (Ryan), D (Dan), or B (both).**

- [B] swim
- [ ] look for shells
- [ ] visit the beach
- [ ] ride a bike
- [ ] skateboard
- [ ] climb trees
- [ ] sail a boat
- [ ] play soccer
- [ ] take photos

Hi Ryan,

I'm visiting my grandma in Italy. We visit her every year, and we fly on a plane. Grandma lives by the beach, and she even has a swimming pool too, so I'm swimming every day! When I'm here, I like riding my bike and looking for shells on the beach. I have a friend named Mario, and his dad has a boat. I'd like to sail the boat, but I can't. The boat is big!

What are you doing on vacation?

Write to me!

Dan

Hi Dan,

I'm at home for vacation, but I'm doing lots of fun things. I'm playing soccer with my friends, skateboarding in the park, and visiting the beach with my mom and my sister (we're swimming and looking for shells). I'd like to go to Italy and eat pizza and ice cream! Are you eating pizza? When we visit my grandma, we take a train. She lives in the city. She doesn't have a swimming pool, but she has a big yard. I like climbing trees and taking photos.

See you soon!

Ryan

1 What do you like doing on vacation? What would you like to do? Make notes.

I like _____
_____
_____

I'd like to _____
_____
_____
_____

2 Write a postcard to Dan. Write about what you are doing on vacation.

Listening: Transportation

1 🎧 15 **Listen and check ✓ the correct picture.**

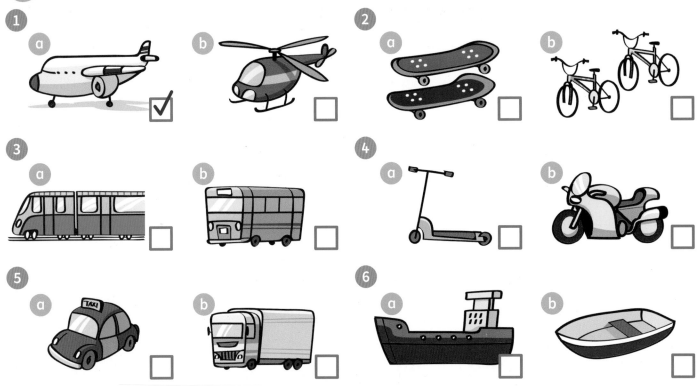

1
a ✓
b

2
a
b

3
a
b

4
a
b

5
a
b

6
a
b

2 🎧 16 **Listen and circle the correct answers.**

1 How does Amelia want to go to China?
   (a) by boat   b by plane

2 Who wants to walk to the sports center?
   a Emma's dad   b Emma

3 What is Ronnie doing?
   a He's playing a computer game.
   b He's playing soccer.

4 What is Ruby doing?
   a She's reading a book.   b She's watching TV.

5 How does Oscar get to school?
   a by car   b by bus

6 Which bus stops next to Laura's house?
   a number 20   b number 12

1 **Look at the photos and mime the actions.**
Play the guessing game.

> Number 2! You're driving a car.

> Yes, I am!

canoe

car

hot-air balloon

train

rocket

motorcycle

2 **Think of an amazing place to visit. Complete the sentences.**

MY AMAZING PLACE

I'd like to go to _____.
I'd like to travel with _____.
I'd like to travel by _____.

3 **Talk about your amazing place.**

> I'd like to go to London. I'd like to travel with my mom, my dad, and my brother. I'd like to travel by hot-air balloon!

LONDON

8 ing Forms

Dancing is great.

Playing volleyball is difficult.

Swimming is fun.

Watching TV is boring.

Language Focus

Use **verb** + **ing** to make sentences describing activities.

Riding is great.

Flying a kite is difficult.

1 **Circle the correct words to complete the sentences.**

1 (Flying) / Fly a kite is difficult.

2 Play / Playing computer games is boring.

3 Making / Makes a cake is fun.

4 Riding / Ride a horse is easy.

5 Reads / Reading a book is great.

6 Painting / Paint pictures is fun.

2 Write the words to complete the sentences.

1

Playing baseball
is boring.

2

_____
is great.

3

_____
is fun.

4

_____
is difficult.

5

_____
is fun.

6

_____
is difficult.

3 Complete the dialogue with the words from the box.

> club   Playing   ~~join~~   Dancing   swimming   boring

Sally Let's **(1)** _____join_____ a club.

Bob That's a great idea. What do you think about dancing?

Sally **(2)** _____ is difficult. I'd like to join the **(3)** _____ club.
What about you?

Bob No. Swimming is **(4)** _____.

Sally I think I'll join the soccer **(5)** _____. You can have fun with
your friends.

Bob OK. **(6)** _____ soccer is great.

like + ing

Language Focus

Use **What ... like doing?** to ask about what activities other people like. Use **I like** + **verb** + **ing** to answer. Use **So do I**, **Me, too**, and **I don't** to give positive and negative short answers.

*What sport do you **like doing?***

I like swimming.   **So do I. / Me, too.**

I like playing soccer.   *I don't.*

---

1 Match the sentences with the pictures.

1 I like swimming.

So do I.   `c`

2 I like playing soccer.

I don't.   ☐

3 I like running.

So do I.   ☐

4 I like playing ping-pong.

I don't.   ☐

2 Circle the correct words to complete the dialogue.

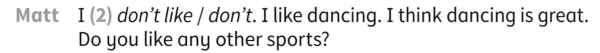

Matt   What sport do you like **(1)** *do* / *doing*?

Jane   I like playing field hockey.

Matt   I **(2)** *don't like* / *don't*. I like dancing. I think dancing is great.
Do you like any other sports?

Jane   Yes, I like **(3)** *rides* / *riding* my bike on a sunny day.

Matt   So **(4)** *do I* / *I do*. I **(5)** *am like* / *like* going to the lake on my bike
and swimming.

Jane   Me, **(6)** *to* / *too*!

3 Look and complete the sentences.

✓ I **like playing tennis**.

✓ So **do I**.

✓ I _____.

✗ I _____.

✓ I _____.

✓ Me _____.

What sport _____?

_____

Reading: A Text Message

1 **Read the messages. Circle the correct words to complete the sentences.**

CHATS School Friends	*Matt, Sally, Ben, You*

Saturday, June 25

I'm at the park at a soccer game. Playing soccer in the park is fun!   **11:32** ✓✓✓

Sally Jones
Hi! Soccer is my favorite sport. Is it for boys and girls? Can I come, too?   **11:35**

Matt Brown
Me, too! Where are you?   **11:40**

Ben Hardy
I don't like soccer. Soccer is boring. I'm playing tennis. See you later.   **11:42**

I'm at the town park near the movie theater. There are 20 boys and girls here. It's on Saturday mornings at 11 o'clock. Come and join us. We are playing in between the ice cream store and the little playground. We're wearing blue T-shirts and yellow shorts.   **11:45** ✓✓✓

Sally Jones
I love that ice cream store! I can't come today. I'm swimming with my sister. Bye!   **11:48**

1 You are at the *swimming pool* / (*park*).

2 Sally *doesn't like* / *likes* soccer.

3 Matt *doesn't like* / *likes* soccer.

4 Ben is playing *soccer* / *tennis.*

5 There are *20* / *11* children playing soccer at the park.

6 Sally is *at the swimming pool* / *eating ice cream.*

1   **Plan a conversation.**

Who are you chatting with? _____

Where are you? _____

Where are your friends? _____

What are you doing? _____

2   **Write your conversation.**

CHATS School Friends

1 🎧 17 **Listen and match the children with the sports they like playing.**

2 🎧 18 **Listen and circle *yes* or *no*.**

1 Tom plays soccer on Fridays.   (yes)/ no
2 Tom plays soccer at a soccer club.   yes / no
3 On Saturdays, Tom goes swimming with his friends.   yes / no
4 For Tom, swimming is boring.   yes / no
5 Tom plays ping-pong on Sundays.   yes / no
6 Tom has a new tennis racket.   yes / no

1 **Work with a friend. What is the equipment? Look, choose, and say.**

Number 5.

They're goggles.

| goal | board | racket | helmet | field | goggles | bat | net |

①

②

③

④

⑤

⑥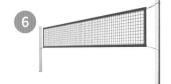

⑦

⑧

2 **With your friend, think of sports that need the equipment in Activity 1. Play the guessing game.**

Do you need a racket?

Yes, you do.

Is it tennis?

No, it isn't.

Is it badminton?

Yes, it is!

3 **Create a sport and draw it. Complete and practice.**

The name of my sport is _____.

You play my sport in / on _____.

For my sport, you need _____.

4 **Talk about your sport.**

The name of my sport is hotball. You play hotball on a court. For my sport, you need two balls and a net.

9 Can for Requests

Can we go hiking this weekend?

Can I go to Lucy's house to listen to music this afternoon?

Can we eat pizza for dinner tomorrow evening?

Language Focus

Use **Can I** / **we** + **verb** to make requests.

Can I go horseback riding tomorrow morning?

Can we visit Grandpa and Grandma in the afternoon?

1 Match to complete the sentences.

1 Can I

2 Can I visit

3 Can we

4 Can I go

5 Can we have

6 Can we take

a my cousin on the weekend?

b horseback riding tomorrow afternoon?

c pizza for dinner?

d go camping in the summer?

e my soccer ball to the park?

f help you in the yard?

2 Complete the dialogues with the words from the box.

> help   visit   ~~what~~   have   Can   We

Dad Tom, **(1)** ___what___ would you like to do on Saturday?

Tom **(2)** _____ we go to the park in the afternoon?

Dad Fine. What about you, Lucy? What would you like to do?

Lucy Can I **(3)** _____ Grandma in the afternoon? I want to **(4)** _____ her in the yard.

Dad OK. **(5)** _____ can go to the park in the morning and to Grandma's in the afternoon. What do you want to eat for dinner?

Tom and Lucy Can we **(6)** _____ pizza?

Dad Yes!

3 Write questions using *Can I* or *Can we* and the words from the box.

> build a tree house   have pizza   ~~have a party~~
> go horseback riding   visit Grandpa   go swimming

1 **Can we have a party** this weekend?

4 _____ for dinner tomorrow afternoon?

2 _____ tomorrow morning?

5 _____ tomorrow morning?

3 _____ tomorrow afternoon?

6 _____ tomorrow afternoon?

Review

Language Focus

Use **Do** to ask Yes/No questions. Use **Can ... ?** to ask about ability. Use question words (**Where** / **Whose**) to ask questions.

Does *your sister eat tomatoes?*	*Yes, she does.*
Do *spiders have eight legs?*	*Yes, they do.*
Can *you swim?*	*No, I can't.*
Where *are my pencils?*	*On the desk.*
Whose *sweater is pink?*	*Emily's.*

1 Read and write the question words.

1 ____Does____ your brother like apples? Yes, he does.

2 _____ you sing? Yes, I can.

3 _____ you have a go-kart? No, I don't.

4 _____ your mom get up at six o'clock? No, she doesn't.

5 _____ bag is this? It's Dan's.

2 **Write questions.**

1 hiking / Mark / Does / like / ? **Does Mark like hiking?** _____

2 socks / these / Whose / are / ? _____

3 horseback riding / Can / go / tomorrow / we / ? _____

4 your / a lot / Does / sleep / cat / ? _____

5 toy store / the / Where / is / ? _____

6 your / a movie theater / town / Does / have / ? _____

3 **Complete the questions.**

1 ____**Can you play**____ volleyball? No, I can't.

2 _____ a train station?
Yes, it does.

3 _____ dancing? Yes, I do.

4 _____ my pens and pencils?
They're in your pencil case.

5 _____ book
_____ ? It's not mine. It's May's.

6 _____ any cheese? No, we don't.

Reading: A Story

1 **Read the story. Answer the questions.**

1 How old is Cinderella? <u>She is young.</u>

2 Who does she live with? _____

3 What time is the party? _____

4 Whose party is it? _____

5 Can the prince find Cinderella? _____

6 Whose feet are the right size for the shoe? _____

Cinderella is a fairy tale about a young girl. She has blue eyes and blond hair. She lives with her two ugly sisters and her wicked stepmother. She gets up early and cleans the house every day. One day, she gets a party invitation. It says:

> Come to a party at the palace on Saturday. It starts at seven o'clock.
>
> Prince Harry

Cinderella asks her wicked stepmother, "Can I go to the party?" but her stepmother says, "No, you can't."

But Cinderella has a fairy godmother. She helps Cinderella get a dress, and she helps her get to the party.

Cinderella is wearing a beautiful dress and shoes. She meets Prince Harry at the party. At twelve o'clock, Cinderella goes home. She runs, and she has only one shoe. The prince says, "Where is Cinderella?"

The next day, the prince looks for Cinderella, but he can't find her. He looks all around town. He has Cinderella's shoe, and he asks the girls in town to try on the shoe.

He goes to Cinderella's house, and her sisters try on the shoe. Their feet aren't small, but the shoe is. Cinderella tries on the shoe, and it fits! Hooray!

Cinderella and the prince live happily ever after.

1 **Put the sentences in order to make the story of *Sleeping Beauty*, a princess who lives in a palace.**

a The wicked witch isn't invited. She is angry. ☐

b When Sleeping Beauty is 16, she cuts her finger on a spinning wheel. ☐

c A prince finds her. The people in the palace wake up. ☐

d She and everyone in the palace sleep for 100 years. ☐

e The wicked witch says, "She will cut her finger and die." ☐

f A forest grows around the palace. ☐

g Sleeping Beauty is a baby. Her parents have a birthday party for her. ☐ 1

2 **Use the sentences from Activity 1 to write the story of *Sleeping Beauty*.**

When Sleeping Beauty is a baby, _____

_____

_____

_____

_____

_____

_____

_____

_____

_____

_____

They all live happily ever after.

Listening: Fun on Vacation

1 🎧 19 **What can Edward do at summer camp?**
Listen and check ☑ or put an X ☒.

This Week at Summer Camp!

Take horseback riding lessons. ☑

Build a tree house. ☐

Swim in the river. ☐

Watch TV. ☐

Go fishing. ☐

Go hiking. ☐

Play volleyball and tennis. ☐

Help in the yard. ☐

2 🎧 20 **Listen and circle the correct answers.**

1 What does Mila want to do now?

　ⓐ go to the beach

　b have lunch

2 Whose house is it?

　a It's Mila's house.

　b It's Grandpa's house.

3 How many bedrooms are there?

　a five

　b four

4 Does the house have a yard?

　a Yes, it does.

　b No, it doesn't.

5 Can Mila go hiking tomorrow?

　a Yes, she can.

　b No, she can't.

6 Who wants to help in the kitchen?

　a Mila's cousins

　b Mila

1 Imagine you are at summer camp. Check ✓ five things you can do. Then ask a friend and check ✓ what you can do at their camp.

> Can you take horseback riding lessons at your summer camp?

> Yes, you can.

● SUMMER CAMP

You can . . .	My Camp	My Friend's Camp
take horseback riding lessons		
build a tree house		
swim		
watch TV		
bake cakes		
play sports		
ride a bike		
read books		
go hiking		
visit new places		

2 Choose one thing from Activity 1 that you and your friend can do at your camps. Draw a picture of you and your friend.

3 Talk about your picture.

> Look. This is me and Liam. We're at summer camp. We're building a tree house!

Audioscripts

Welcome Unit page 10

1 Boy Hello! This is my new classroom. Come and look. This is the board! We have a big board!

2 Boy There's a nice clock on the wall. It's red. Can you see it?

3 Boy This is the teacher's desk. Look. There are some rulers on the desk.

4 Boy Can you see the bookcase? There are some books in it. I want to read them!

5 Boy This is my desk. I sit here with my friend, Ben. There are two chairs: one chair for me and one chair for Ben.

6 Boy Look! This is my new pencil case. There are some crayons in my pencil case. My crayons are new, too!

Ms. White	Good morning, everyone!
Children	Good morning, Ms. White.
Ms. White	It's nice to see you all again! Do you like the new classroom?
Children	Yes, we do!
Ms. White	Me, too! OK! Oh, no. Don't sit down. Don't sit down, please. Stand up. Stand up, please. Can you get your books? Get your books, please. That's great. Now, open your books to page one. Oh, no. Don't get your crayons. Don't get your crayons. Get a pencil and write your name. Write your name, please. That's very good. Good job, class!

Unit 1 page 18

Hello! I'm Lucy, and I have a big sister, Eva. I love my big sister. Do you want to know about her day? OK. Eva gets up at six o'clock. Six o'clock is early! Then she gets dressed and helps Mom make breakfast. Eva has breakfast at seven o'clock. After breakfast, she brushes her teeth and puts her books in her bag. At eight o'clock, Eva goes to school. Then she has lunch at one o'clock. Chicken and carrots are her favorite! After school, Eva plays with me. Then we have dinner together at seven o'clock, and we go to bed at nine o'clock. In bed, Eva and I talk about our day. That's one of my favorite things!

Teacher	OK, it's your turn, Dan. When do you get home from school?
Dan	I get home at four o'clock. I walk home with my mom and my sister. My dad's at work.
Teacher	That sounds nice. And what do you do at home?
Dan	I play with my sister. Then, at five o'clock we go to the park. I play in the park with friends.
Teacher	That's good! And when do you have dinner?
Dan	Hmm . . . Well, I get home from the park at seven o'clock, and I have dinner at eight o'clock. After dinner, my sister and I read a story with my dad. We like stories!
Teacher	A story after dinner is great! And then do you go to bed?
Dan	No, I don't! I brush my teeth, and then I go to bed.
Teacher	Oh, of course, Dan! Good job!

Unit 2 page 26

Hello! Today, I'm at the zoo with my friends! There's Alex. He's with the tigers. Alex loves tigers. Oh, look. That's Grace. Grace likes tigers too, but her favorite animal is the hippo. For Grace, hippos are fantastic! Now, can you see the crocodiles? My friend Tom is next to them. Tom likes crocodiles a lot. And that's my friend Kim. Kim likes crocodiles too, but snakes are her favorite animal. Kim likes all snakes, long or short, big or small! And my friend Jill is there, with the zebras. Zebras are Jill's favorite animal. OK, what about me? I'm Nick, and I love polar bears! Polar bears are amazing!

Tony	Hello, Holly!
Holly	Oh! Hi, Tony!
Tony	Are you here with your family?
Holly	Yes, I am. We really like the zoo.
Tony	I like it, too. The crocodiles are amazing!
Holly	Yes! My mom really likes crocodiles. They're her favorite. My dad doesn't like crocodiles. He loves zebras. Zebras are my dad's favorite animal.
Tony	Zebras are great! What about your brother? What's his favorite animal?
Holly	Well, my brother likes snakes! Arghh!
Tony	Haha! I love snakes, too. They're cool!
Holly	No, they're not! I don't like snakes, and my sister doesn't like snakes. They're ugly!
Tony	OK, OK. Hey, do you like parrots, Holly? They're my favorite.
Holly	Hmm . . . not really. I don't like parrots, Tony. I like monkeys! Monkeys are funny!

Unit 3 page 34

Sam	Do you like your town, Hugo?
Hugo	Yes, I do! It's great. Do you like your town, Sam?
Sam	Yes. My town is very nice. It has a new café! Does your town have a café, Hugo?
Hugo	Yes, it does. It's called The Blue Café. We go there for breakfast on the weekend.

Sam	Cool! My town has a big movie theater. Does your town have a movie theater?
Hugo	No, it doesn't. There isn't a movie theater in my town.
Sam	Then come to my town! And I can go to the swimming pool in your town, Hugo.
Hugo	That's right, Sam. My town has a great swimming pool!
Sam	Yes, it's fun! My town doesn't have a swimming pool. But it has a big playground.
Hugo	My town has a big playground, too. It's next to the train station. Does your town have a train station, Sam?
Sam	No, it doesn't. There isn't a train station in my town. I can go to your town by car!
Hugo	Good idea!

🎧 08

1 Boy	Hello. Can you help me, please?
Girl	Yes, of course.
Boy	Where's the bookstore?
Girl	It's next to the clothing store.
Boy	OK, next to the clothing store. Thanks!
2 Girl	Hi, Eric. We're at the bus station.
Eric	Where's the bus station?
Girl	It's behind the museum.
Eric	Behind the museum. OK. See you soon!
3 Boy	Where's the zoo, May?
May	Hmm . . . let's look at the map. The zoo is in front of the school.
Boy	Great! Let's go!
4 Girl	Hello. Do you know the monument?
Boy	Yes, I do.
Girl	Where is it?
Boy	It's on the hill. Look!
Girl	Yes! I can see it on the hill!
5 Boy	Are you at the sports center, Sophie?
Sophie	Yes, I am.
Boy	Is it behind the parking lot?
Sophie	No, it's next to the parking lot.
Boy	Next to the parking lot? OK, see you there!

Unit 4 page 42

🎧 09

1 Polly	What's in the cabinet, Tim?
Tim	There are some potatoes.
Polly	Some potatoes? Is that all? Let's go to the market!
2 Tim	Would you like an egg sandwich, Polly?
Polly	Yes, please! Are there any eggs?
Tim	Yes, there are some eggs in the fridge.
3 Polly	Are there any lemons, Tim?
Tim	Yes, there are. How many lemons would you like?
Polly	Hmm . . . I'd like three lemons, please.
4 Polly	OK. We need some vegetables for the salad.
Tim	Look! There are some beans in the fridge.
Polly	That's right! We have lots of beans!

5 Tim	What's your favorite fruit, Polly?
Polly	Hmm . . . I love watermelon.
Tim	Great. Would you like some watermelon after lunch?
Polly	Yes, please!
6 Polly	Tim, would you like some pizza?
Tim	Yes, good idea!
Polly	OK. We have some cheese. Are there any tomatoes?
Tim	Yes, there are. The tomatoes are on the table. Look.
Polly	OK. Great!

10

1 Dad	Would you like a kiwi, Lucy?
Lucy	Hmm. No thanks, Dad. Are there any grapes?
Dad	Yes, there are.
Lucy	I'd like some grapes, please.
2 Mom	Would you like an apple, Connor?
Connor	No, thank you, Mom. Can I have a kiwi?
Mom	Let's see . . . Oh, yes, there's a kiwi here. Here you go.
Connor	Thanks, Mom.
3 Anna	Where's my lunchbox, Dad?
Dad	I don't know, Anna. What would you like?
Anna	My apple. Oh, my lunchbox is here. And here's my apple!
Dad	Good!
4 Mom	Jack?
Jack	Yes, Mom.
Mom	Can you help me, please? I can't find the mangoes.
Jack	Look, Mom. The mangoes are in the fridge. Would you like one?
Mom	Yes, please!
5 Dad	Are you sure, May?
May	Yes, Dad. I'd like some for breakfast. Please!
Dad	OK. Let's get it. It's a big watermelon!
May	Thanks, Dad. I like watermelon!

Unit 5 page 50

🎧 11

1 Milly	Wow! These mirrors are pretty!
Mom	Yes! Would you like this blue mirror or that orange mirror?
Milly	I'd like this blue mirror. Thanks, Mom.
2 Milly	There are lots of closets, Mom!
Mom	Yes, there are. What about this one, Milly?
Milly	Hmm . . . It's nice, but it's very small.
Mom	OK. Let's get that closet. It's big!
Milly	Good idea!
3 Milly	I like those rugs, Mom!
Mom	Me, too. Do you want the red one or the green one?
Milly	Can we get the red rug, please?
Mom	Of course! Red is your favorite color!
4 Milly	Look at these lamps! The yellow lamp is ugly.
Mom	Yes, it is. What about this white lamp?
Milly	I like this white lamp! It's nice for my new bedroom!

5	**Mom**	Look at these couches, Milly. I like this purple couch.
	Milly	I like the purple couch, too, Mom. The brown couch isn't very nice.
6	**Milly**	Mom, can we get a poster of an animal for my bedroom?
	Mom	Good idea. Look at the crocodile!
	Milly	It's cool, but I love the tiger.
	Mom	OK, let's get the poster of the tiger!

	Dad	Look at this bedroom! You two need to clean it up.
	Children	Sorry, Dad.
	Dad	Whose ball is this?
	Adam	That's Lucy's ball.
	Dad	Can you put your ball in the box, please, Lucy?
	Lucy	OK, Dad.
	Dad	Whose crayons are these?
	Adam	They're Lucy's crayons, too, Dad.
	Dad	OK. Lucy, put your crayons in the pencil case, please. Now, jeans! Are these your jeans, too, Lucy?
	Lucy	No, they're Adam's jeans.
	Dad	Put your jeans in the closet, please, Adam.
	Adam	OK.
	Dad	And Adam . . . your jacket's on the chair again!
	Adam	That's Lucy's jacket, Dad.
	Lucy	Oh! Sorry! Yes, it's my jacket. I can put it in the closet.
	Dad	Good job. Now, whose books are these, Lucy?
	Lucy	They're Adam's books, Dad.
	Dad	Adam, put these books on your desk, please.
	Adam	OK. But Lucy's kite is on my desk, Dad. Look.
	Dad	Lucy's kite? Lucy, your kite goes in the box!
	Lucy	OK, Dad.
	Dad	Good job, children! Now you have a clean bedroom again!

Unit 6 page 58

1	**Grace**	Happy birthday, Jill! What time is your party?
	Jill	Thanks, Grace! It's at five o'clock. I'm very excited!
2	**Dad**	Are you OK, Jenny?
	Jenny	Dad, the party's great. But I'm very tired now.
	Dad	You're tired, and it's late. Let's go home.
3	**Max**	I'm very happy, Leah!
	Leah	Why?
	Max	Look. I got new glasses for my birthday.
	Leah	Oh, yes! Your new glasses are cool, Max!
4	**Kate**	Henry, are you OK?
	Henry	No, I'm not. I'm very angry. Look. Carmen's party is on Friday, and my party is on Friday, too!
	Kate	Oh, no!
5	**Mom**	Oliver, are you scared?
	Oliver	Yes, Mom. I'm scared. I don't like that big spider . . .
	Mom	Oh, don't worry, Oliver. The spider is Dad!
6	**Beth**	Dad, it's Jamie's party today . . .

	Dad	That's great, Beth. But you look sad.
	Beth	I am sad. Jamie's party is in the park, and it's raining!
	Dad	Oh, I see!

Hello, my name's Alice. I love birthday parties. They're fun! We can play with our friends and eat cake. This year, there are lots of parties in my class. And they are all different. Alex and Dan's party is in January. Their party is at our town's new movie theater. They're very excited! Then we have Kim's party in March. She's very happy, too. Kim's party is at her family's farm! I love animals! Now, Pat and Mark's birthdays are in April. And their party is at the sports center! They like playing sports. Then Bobby's party is in May. It's at the Sunshine Café. We love the cake there! And lastly, my party is with my friend Olivia. Our birthdays are in June, and our party is in the park!

Unit 7 page 66

1	**Girl**	Look, Michael. I'm flying my plane. What are you doing? Are you flying your helicopter?
	Michael	No, I'm not. Look. I'm flying my plane, too!
2	**Boy**	Come on, Kelly. Let's go! We can take our skateboards.
	Kelly	I don't want to ride my skateboard. I'd like to ride my bike.
	Boy	OK! Let's take our bikes!
3	**Boy**	Mom, I'd like to take the train to the movie theater.
	Mom	Me, too. But the train doesn't stop at the movie theater. Let's take the bus.
	Boy	OK. Let's go by bus.
4	**Girl**	Would you like to ride a motorcycle, Nick?
	Nick	Hmm . . . I'm not sure. Motorcycles are very big. I'd like to ride a scooter.
	Girl	Really?
	Nick	Yes. My scooter is great!
5	**Boy**	Does your dad drive a truck, Ava?
	Ava	No, he doesn't.
	Boy	What does he drive?
	Ava	My dad drives a taxi.
6	**Girl**	Look, Tom! Would you like to get on that big ship or on that little boat?
	Tom	I'd like to get on that little boat.
	Girl	Why?
	Tom	Little boats are fun!

1	**Boy**	Look at all these countries, Amelia. Where would you like to go?
	Amelia	I'd like to go to China.
	Boy	Well, you'd need to take a plane.
	Amelia	Not a plane. I'd like to go to China by boat!
	Boy	By boat? Wow! But China is far!
2	**Emma**	Dad, can we ride our bikes to the sports center?
	Dad	That's a nice idea, but there are lots of cars on the road, Emma. Let's walk.
	Emma	Oh, Dad. I don't want to walk . . .
	Dad	Come on, Emma. We can walk fast! The sports center isn't far.

3	**Lola**	Hi, Ronnie.
	Ronnie	Oh, hi, Lola.
	Lola	What are you doing?
	Ronnie	I'm playing a computer game. It's about cars!
	Lola	Would you like to play soccer with me?
	Ronnie	OK. When I finish my game.
4	**Ruby**	Hello, Ted.
	Ted	Hi, Ruby. What are you doing?
	Ruby	I'm watching TV. What about you?
	Ted	I'm reading a book about planes. It's amazing!
5	**Girl**	Do you go to school by car, Oscar?
	Oscar	No, I don't.
	Girl	Do you walk?
	Oscar	No, I don't. I take the bus to school.
6	**Ben**	How do I get to your house, Laura?
	Laura	Take the bus, Ben.
	Ben	The number twelve bus?
	Laura	No, take the number twenty. The twenty stops next to my house.
	Ben	OK!

Unit 8 page 74

 17

1	**Boy**	Do you like playing baseball, Chloe?
	Chloe	Yes, I love baseball! It's fun!
2	**Girl**	Noah, would you like to play ping-pong with me?
	Noah	Yes, of course! Playing ping-pong is great!
3	**Boy**	What sports do you like, Jess?
	Jess	Well, I like playing one sport. You play it with a racket. Guess.
	Boy	That's easy! Tennis.
	Jess	No, I like playing badminton!
4	**Girl**	What do you think about soccer, Lucas?
	Lucas	Playing soccer is boring! I like playing volleyball.
	Girl	Me, too. Playing volleyball is fun.
5	**Boy**	OK. We can play field hockey or soccer, Esme.
	Esme	Playing field hockey is difficult. I like soccer.
	Boy	OK! Let's play soccer!
6	**Girl**	Are you ready for the game, Ethan?
	Ethan	Yes, I am! I love playing field hockey! Field hockey's my favorite sport!

 18

Hello! I'm Tom, and I love playing sports. They're great!
On Fridays, I play soccer with my friends. We go to a soccer club. We wear red T-shirts at our soccer club. On Saturdays, I go swimming with my family. Swimming is fun! There's a new swimming pool next to my house, and I love it. On Sundays, I play ping-pong with my brother. Playing ping-pong is easy! Oh, and I play tennis, too! There's a nice tennis court in the park in our town. I like playing on it. Oh, I can show you my new tennis racket. It's purple and blue! Look!

Unit 9 page 82

 19

Edward	Mr. Thompson, can I ask you some questions about summer camp?
Mr. Thompson	Yes, of course you can, Edward.
Edward	OK. Can I take horseback riding lessons this week?
Mr. Thompson	Yes, you can. You can take horseback riding lessons every morning with Ellie. She's very friendly.
Edward	Great! And can I build a tree house?
Mr. Thompson	Good news, Edward. You can build a tree house tomorrow morning!
Edward	That's fun! You know, I really like swimming. Can I go swimming in the river?
Mr. Thompson	Sorry. You can't swim in the river, Edward. But you can swim in our swimming pool.
Edward	OK. And can I watch TV this week?
Mr. Thompson	Oh, no, you can't. We don't have TVs at the camp! There are lots of things to do outside. You can go fishing and hiking this week.
Edward	Well, fishing and hiking are OK . . . Hmm . . . Can I play volleyball and tennis, too?
Mr. Thompson	No, you can't. Not this week. But you can help in the yard.
Edward	OK. I like helping!

 20

Mila	I love this house, Mom. Look out of the window. There's the ocean. It's big. It's amazing!
Mom	Yes, it is, Mila!
Mila	Can we go to the beach now?
Mom	Hmm . . . Not now. Let's have lunch. We can go to the beach after that. OK?
Mila	OK!
Mom	You know, Grandpa's very happy that you, your cousins, and I are staying in his house.
Mila	Yes, I like being in Grandpa's beach house. And I like playing with my cousins!
Mom	I can see that!
Mila	Grandpa's house is big, Mom. How many bedrooms are there? Four or five?
Mom	Four. There are four bedrooms.
Mila	My favorite thing about the house is the yard.
Mom	Yes, the yard is nice. Would you like to help Grandpa in the yard this week?
Mila	Yes, of course! I'd like that. And Mom, can we go hiking tomorrow?
Mom	Yes, of course we can. We can go with your cousins. Now, what about lunch? Can you help me make it?
Mila	Yes! I love helping in the yard, and I love helping in the kitchen!

Acknowledgments

The authors and publishers acknowledge the following sources of copyright material and are grateful for the permissions granted. While every effort has been made, it has not always been possible to identify the sources of all the material used, or to trace all copyright holders. If any omissions are brought to our notice, we will be happy to include the appropriate acknowledgments on reprinting and in the next update to the digital edition, as applicable.

Key: ST = Starter, U = Unit

Photography

The following images are sourced from Getty Images.

ST: recep-bg/E+; goldenKB/iStock/Getty Images Plus; **U1:** Comstock Images/Stockbyte; Studiocartoon/iStock/GettyImages Plus; Wavebreakmedia Ltd/Getty Images Plus; **U2:** Dinodia Photo/The Image Bank Unreleased; Marka/Universal Images Group; wilpunt/iStock/Getty Images Plus; Skyler Ewing/EyeEm; real444/iStock/Getty Images Plus; Juanmonino/iStock/Getty Images Plus; Nophamon Yanyapong/EyeEm; ValuaVitaly/iStock/Getty Images Plus; nattanan726/iStock/Getty Images Plus; DrPAS/iStock/Getty Images Plus; anankkml/iStock/Getty Images Plus; zokru/iStock/Getty Images Plus; VitalisG/iStock/Getty Images Plus; AaronAmat/iStock/Getty Images Plus; Image Source/Vetta; Kuntalee Rangnoi/iStock/Getty Images Plus; Andreas Speich/EyeEm; Js Photography/Moment; Piotr Pestka/500px; WLDavies/iStock/Getty Images Plus; Razvan Ciuca/Moment; FatCamera/E+; **U3:** selimaksan/E+; Jose Luis Pelaez Inc/DigitalVision; Lena Granefelt; **U4:** alex5248/iStock/Getty Images Plus; Devonyu/iStock/Getty Images Plus; kbwills/iStock/Getty Images Plus; Kangah/iStock/Getty Images Plus; Scrambled/iStock/Getty Images Plus; Paola Zucchi/Photolibrary/Getty Images Plus; Moncherie/E+; Jose Luis Pelaez Inc/DigitalVision; Soldt/iStock/Getty Images Plus; Juanmonino/E+; ozgurdonmaz/iStock/Getty Images Plus; Jodie Griggs/Moment; SvetlanaK/iStock/Getty Images Plus; subjug/iStock/Getty Images Plus; Natthakan Jommanee/EyeEm; Jamakosy/iStock/Getty Images Plus; pjohnson1/E+; Imgorthand/E+; **U5:** Stephanie Hager - HagerPhoto/Stockbyte; irina88w/iStock/Getty Images Plus; Maskot; Iwan Chorniy/iStock/Getty Images Plus; cyfrogclone/DigitalVision Vectors; **U6:** David Marsden/Photolibrary/Getty Images Plus; Creativ Studio Heinemann; 130920/Moment; Tolimir/E+; Craig Tuttle/Corbis Historical; View Pictures/Universal Images Group; Alain BENAINOUS/Gamma-Rapho; kali9/E+; **U7:** pikenpri foto/Moment; MHJ/DigitalVision Vectors; Oscar Porras González/500px/500Px Plus; Cassandra Kosmayer/EyeEm; James Hipps/EyeEm; New SIGHT Photography/iStock/Getty Images Plus; Stocktrek Images; Henn Photography/Cultura; Rakdee/DigitalVision Vectors; Matriyoshka/iStock/Getty Images Plus; **U8:** Cybernesco/iStock/Getty Images Plus; carlosalvarez/E+; Goodboy Picture Company/E+; Layland Masuda/Moment Open; Elena Riim/EyeEm; Daniel MacDonald/www.dmacphoto.com/Moment; fstop123/iStock/Getty Images Plus; Stockbyte; Andersen Ross Photography Inc/DigitalVision; Tim Macpherson/Cultura; ddukang/iStock/Getty Images Plus; freestylephoto/iStock/Getty Images Plus; artisteer/iStock/Getty Images Plus; Thomas Northcut/Photodisc; Viruj/iStock/Getty Images Plus; Nerthuz/iStock/Getty Images Plus; ZargonDesign/E+; Bim/E+; **U9:** Imgorthand/E+; Jupiterimages/Creatas; wundervisuals/E+.

The following images are sourced from another library.

U4: Andy Tu/Shutterstock; U8: Mike Flippo/Shutterstock; tkemot/Shutterstock.

Commissioned photography by Stephen Bond.

Illustrations

Clive Goodyer (Beehive Illustration); Anna Hancock (Beehive Illustration); Andrew Hennessy; Marek Jagucki; Chris Lensch; Daniel Limon (Beehive Illustration); Bernice Lum; Andy Parker; Alan Rowe (Beehive Illustration); David Russell; David Semple.

Audio

Audio production by John Marshall Media.

Typeset

EMC Design limited.

Cover design by We Are Bold.